Selected Poems

BRAD DREW

Selected Poems

1973 to 2022

BARDDRIEV PRESS

First Edition
Casebound Hardcover

ISBN: 978-0-6454701-2-3

Layout, Cover and Book Design: Brad Drew
Drawings and prints by Brad Drew

Frontispiece: 'Self Portrait, 1983.'
Quill liner & Indian Ink on Fabriano Paper.

PROLOGUE

I suddenly come to realise that my modest journey towards a poetic ideal has been taking place for what is now, fast approaching five decades. The passage of those decades has been at times, both fitful and erratic, from that first impulse to give voice in a matter of the heart - which in an instant, opened the door to a wider world of expression, previously engaged in, only as an academic necessity in the course of higher schooling but not fully appreciated back in those early years. In that moment, came the realisation that the balancing acts possible with arranging words, made for a very special magic and that I did have some innate sense for selection and arrangement.

In these beginnings, I must confess, I was heavily influenced by the lyrics of a number of the more popular (but also specially talented), more acutely soulful, songwriters of those early seventies years, who tapped into the hearts of the youthful, and not quite so, in search of love and heartache and heartbreak. And they were poetic - and they made sense and carried meaning to those of us taking our first steps down those sometimes-lost paths. My first steps, in retrospect, were naive at very best but they opened the way to an awareness, to a conscious acknowledgement of all those phrases which can sometimes drop out of nowhere into one's head and sound just right ... and one thinks, 'That's really good. I could make something of that. I must mark it down before it gets lost in the daylight.'

Some time again would pass, before I joyfully discovered Dylan Thomas - as I myself, relocated for a significant period (in many more ways than one) to his own hemisphere of the world ... And became an ardent admirer for life. He is recorded as wishing to write poetry from the very beginning because he had fallen in love with words: with their shapes and sounds, their music and colours. Much of his work carries a level of obscurity, which even a number of his editors have found elusive at times; but the music which he creates from the English language, with 'words', transcends any need to fully comprehend everything contained therein – a reading in itself, leaves one with a tangible emotional impact, which often asks for nothing more. The pieces are so wonderfully disciplined and illusively clever in that, on closer examination, one realises that there is most often, a rhyming scheme present which is seldom obvious at all – and yet, it is almost always there.

This cleverness is an aspect which has always appealed to me – the indirectness, the use of metaphor and allegory, rhyme which is not necessarily obvious: the poetry which shows itself obliquely, from both the eye and ear's peripheral viewpoint –an ideal to which to aspire but one to never be equaled. But we try ... and sometimes feel some small satisfaction with our fledgling efforts.

At this point, I must acknowledge two other, singular masters who have continued to feed my extended appetite for the pursuit of 'the poem'. A list of truly-memorable poets throughout history is, in itself, almost endless – but there are two figures who stand out for me, aside from their own creations, as instrumental in awaking the broader consciousness of poetry itself. Clive James, apart from his own incandescent contributions, produced a number of collections of wonderful essays about other poets – finally contributing shortly before his passing, a beautiful collection of 'roughly eighty poems' (with his usual erudite commentaries), entitled 'The Fire of Joy'. And, for the most knowledgeable, all-round, hugely-entertaining reference work for the aspiring poet, is Stephen Fry's 'The Ode Less Travelled', accompanied by the continuous insertion of his own terribly clever examples of each poetic point under discussion.

And at the end of the day, Thomas for myself, continues as my yardstick by which all else is eventually measured.

And so, for very almost five decades, I have striven to write an occasional poem ... not just 'poetry', but 'a poem'. There have been flurries of great intensity, separated by the occasional moments (sometimes great tracts) of dearth, the greater of which, once swallowed up two of those decades in one large gulp. They had been preceded by a firm and sound, formative period and fortunately, were eventually followed by times of increasingly-conscious development of what sometimes revealed itself as a small mastery of sorts. It was perhaps no accident but rather, an act of fate, that the second, increasingly-developed period was initially precipitated by the return of one very special muse, from the much earlier period in London. It is at this point, more than ever before, that the poetic consciousness kicks in ... And as one further muse, the ultimate, in time emerges, there comes a time when poetry grows in its scope as never before.

Over the wealth of years intervening, the sum total of poetry and poems grew considerably and inevitably were assembled in a sort of collected works, interspersed with a similarly-eclectic assemblage of personal artworks: drawings and prints produced across a similar time span and beyond. In retrospect, this perhaps made of one book, an overwhelming onslaught ... pretty perhaps, but too much to digest in any number of sittings for most ... and so, a production more likely to languish forever on one's bookshelf – a curiosity.

The collection is quite eclectic in its subject matter, style and expansiveness, ranging from some very long endeavours to the briefest of haiku, tanka and other short poems. With this current collection of personally selected poems, a necessary culling has taken place, hopefully reducing the offering to one which I, at least, consider to be a sound collection of the better pieces to have emerged over time.

Brad Drew
November 2022

THE POEMS

THE WISE AMONG US

The wise among us shun love,
green fields and distant skies.
The wise will live and breathe each day
as the cow chews endless cud ...
Their ways are simple and direct;
their lives tick steadily by the clock
towards that same, inevitable end ...
But then, the wise have never loved.

'The City Sleeps'
Graphos pen with Indian Ink on Ingres Paper, 1973.

EVENING

Quiet now, as city lights glitter
and a barge moves slowly upstream;
factory lights fall on deaf waters
while cars move by: an endless stream
to pause at traffic lights outside my window.
One lone breeze stirs,
barely moving trees outside
nor the light above my table.
Perhaps tomorrow will be cooler ...

These days move slowly;
the nights so fast,
impatient to feel the dawn.
Nights carry oneness pervading,
bringing the start of new days –
peace, excitement, and cool.
The days exert their controls
as nights offer freedoms and love ...
companionships to indulge:
music, theatre, dinners
fresh air, darkness, lights and bed.
Another world ... and life.

PUTNEY BRIDGE

I loved you
Oh! So well, that summer ...
and tonight, a girl stood by me
on Putney Bridge in rain,
waiting for the bus and looking
so very much like you.
I almost answered to her eye.
Only, she may have not been you
and of that, I was afraid.

I stood there with your phantom
in two years of distant rain
and that last of summer's
dimming traffic glow ...
let one bus first and then another
go lumbering on their ways;
waiting to mull upon your memory
for just a little further.

And I sit here still ...
on this steaming, empty bus
in this empty, London night
while tears of rain
sweep down moist-lidded windows;
weep monsoons of memories
of one far-distant summer's night ...
abandoned to the damp embrace
of a steamy bus and the hissing kiss
of slick wet tires –
while Cloverdale Park Nursery
seems so very far away.

YOU HAVE NOT CHANGED

You have not changed ...
And winds that bore you from me
on sails of neon men-of-war, full-thrust
past tides of cities, lit with efflorescent beads
of dew in time-shined spores;
have kept you ... I, the wind-flyer.

You have not changed ...
And I, the firefly and moth of constant dreams
and shifting sands: these fluxing tides surging
in the glow of ancient keeps
built high on wave-strewn coastlines;
have kept you ... I, the wind-flyer.

You have not changed ...
And clouds that bore you in me light as dusk
by distant slopes of stream-swept jade
to glide on shining sleds of glass
fresh-honed from Chartres' ancient rose;
have kept you ... I, the born-on-wind.

You have not changed –
And youthful blooms in forest depths
light with their fires, the phoenix keep
fanned high by winds that bore you to me;
sails that kept you ... You, the wind-rider.

'The Embankment, London'

Rollerball & Wash on Arches Paper, 2015

THE KEEPER

The keeper is lost.
And losing, so this unsheathed ring -
Time's annulary, bared in solemn gambit
gambled for an unseen queen ...
She rings the pealing
of the hours and houri, measured out upon
the bane Achilles held.
She keeps, and holding,
holds his unkeeped heart
and bares it to the light of day.

The keeper is lost.
And keeping, keeps his solaced keep:
Kept high on castled crags, between the distance
of his bursting soul's intent.
In his watch-housed sleep
he's marked her measures ...
Timed her hours of queen-shod waking.
For the outlawed swain, Astarte weep -
for he's pawned his heart
and bears it from the light of day.

TRAIN:
EIGHT-THIRTY PADDINGTON
TO PLYMOUTH

Eight-thirty train to Exeter ...
Two hours and forty minutes:
Reading – Taunton – Exeter St Davids.
What's Plymouth?

England slipping by in nameless haze
as the Inter-City knife-slice pulses ::
throbs :: and penetrates :: in lengthy intercourse
over rolling Devon fields ...
And holdings, cottages and barns,
hedgerows, fences, stiles and downs;
battling greenery, striving on by waterways and trees.

Pulsing :: throbbing ::
coursing down these thighs of Noble England.
Grey! Grey blankets draped;
draped in loose soiled folds caressing,
clinging these recumbent loins ...
Ecstasy of the Eight-thirty
Paddington-to-Plymouth.

Second lunge-thrust of the day,
slipping smoothly down, day-long ...
Coming :: Coming :: Oh! I'm coming!
Rape of England!
'LIBS THROW A SPANNER', read the headlines.
On Her back and I'm here, languishing
in Inter-City come.

Black-faced sheep, cottages
and rolling fields, forever.
Ah! ... A junkyard!
Scrapped and beat-up, dented,
battered, rusted, rotting cars:
How quaint! But where's Spring?
And where are you, my Love?

Trees burning ... Burning-out
on sheltered side of hill
and Mother's home
with children playing at her knees;
tends the kitchen;
keeps the home fires burning
while Father's burning tree stumps on the hill.

Embers glow in mist-swathed morning;
lunch approaching;
Father's coming ... All is well
and England lives.

Spring coming :: blankets hugging ::
British Rail's swollen member throbs;
throbs on through the South-West
under blankets, dirtied by its countless comes.

Wasn't it good, My Love? My Loves?
You whom I loved and love ...
I bear you with me, as we make it ::
sigh and make it :: sigh and brake it ::
braking it :: in Taunton.

Spread-out under milky skies;
stretched from star to star ...
There :: here ...
We were frozen :: there :: forever ...
In moments :: that were :: before they :: that are ...
And I am locked here :: now ...
As I have been :: Will be ...

Thudding :: pounding :: throbbing ::
pulsing :: post-Taunton Blues ...
Oh God! I'm coming!
Tadpole legionnaire, I've closed the ranks.
St David's discharge and I'm gone:
just another spunky frog, lost-in-action ...
Exeter, thirty-first day of March, Nineteen-seventy-seven.

THE FISHER SWAIN

Exiled heart and outlawed swain.
Each night: a year – he dreamt in vain;
dreamt of longing and desire –
each night: a year;
each day: a fire.
Seven and-one-half millennia
thus, he dreamt: the Keeper-lost ...
So great the cost of unseen queen, of all she meant
and so, he dreamt.
Astarte wept –

For his pawned heart wept.
And weeping, hid it from the light of day.
With distanced, bursting soul's intent
the queen-shod nightly pealing rent
one heart in two; kept one half and all its healing ...
Bell-keeper and Time's broker;
Bearer of Fate's annulary,
bared in silence long ago ...
Solemn gambit, unseen queen.
Astarte wept –

Whose the tolling; whom the weeping;
whose the dreaming; whom the sleeping?
Distanced in his bursting soul, he slept
and dreamt ... And dreaming, dreamt
of being lost and all it cost.
Sleeping thus, he dreamt once more –

Hours and houri lost to sight –
the years sweep by in endless flight.
The beat of wings drowns out his plight;
their beating lulls his sleep at night,
quells his dreams, his quest for life.
To still the throngs who storm his gates,
Penelope-like, he undertakes to knit
a shawl: a home, a cairn ...
And knitting thus, some gesture make
to quench this thirst which will not slake.
And once, he dreamt –

Waking, dreamt he saw her yet;
knew that he could not forget
her face, her form, her inner light ...
Her sight and sound, that burned so bright and burning,
put his soul to flight, forever owning all his nights.
Astarte slept –

Sleeping thus, his heart she kept.
Of purpose lost, of fire bereft,
he put away his joys and slept;
wounded with a toxin deep
he sought some solace in his sleep ...
Queen-shod pealing in the night:
grail-quest fire that burned so bright
and wound complete, he saw her yet;
wondered then would she forget
one brief, one flaring light.
Astarte slept –

Eternity, he dreams and sleeps:
sweet sleep, this opiate to his days.
He knits his shawl and seeks a way
to find some meaning to his fate;
the wound he would if could, negate.
Another place, he saw the gleam;
tried to forget what might have been ...
To put away, both soul and mind
believing that with friends and time:
distractions of another kind,
his wound would heal and slowly bind.

The world he sought, whilst mainly good,
had not the test of time withstood:
the rigours of a heart bereft.
The friends he gained, pained for his plight
and heard his emptiness at night.
Besieged by calls of night-shod queen,
core of whom he once had been;
the span of which, however slight
he'd been her passion for one night ...
Or two, or three, or more?

He'd made no count; he'd kept no score.
It had not really mattered then ...
Could it have been thus, truly been
little more than simply dream:
illusion of a heart grown sore;
an apparition, once he'd seen?
In constancy, Astarte slept –

And sleeping still, she gave no sign;
no word of queen or how, her life.
If only once for him she'd called
and given purpose to his shawl,
his shroud: for thus it seemed.
Bereft of purpose and of queen,
he hid in darkness, growing dim: apothecary's dream.
But still, forlorn Astarte slept ...
While swain, cleft from his dreams, bereft,
pondered queen; her life.

Her life! He'd never questioned,
for with beauty and the joys she brought
could not come pain with burden fraught.
How could she suffer, ever bright,
when love and beauty were her right?
In reading now, his last refrain
from long ago: a poem called 'Train' ...
He shakes with dawning and alarm;
perhaps was he, had done her harm;
had left an accidental scar
she carried with her from afar –

That onetime, sometime: distant past,
he'd loved and had been loved by her.
Could something there, have led her feet
to flee to Devon, in retreat?
Or was that verse, mere prophesy
of chance but nothing more?
Astarte stirs –

'Foolish swain', Astarte chides.
'That you might ponder so – you're dreaming.
That you with her, could leave some meaning;
lead her somehow to that place;
place her in a state of grace,
longing likewise for your face?
You're mad! It's nothing more than fate!'

But what if, more than poem-forsook,
it led her to the course she took?
And coursing so, you would not know.
You'd thought her gone: another's queen;
her destiny and yours unseen.
You would have followed, had it been.
Astarte wakes –

* * *

What is her wound, this Fisher Queen?
What hurt? What pain? What sorrow; spleen?
He senses it and feels its chill: this malady she suffers still.
She flees in terror and alarm,
afraid that he might do her harm.
What harm was done he cannot know
and so, he curses mind so slow:
so thick, that he might never grasp
the depth or meaning of his task.
Astarte wakes and rises –

What if these cups they seek, were one ...
Both wounds to share and overcome;
in constancy their hurts to spare;
in loving and with caring, where
one grail for both becomes.
Astarte placed grails in two hearts
hiding them in distant parts;
waiting for a time to come
when destiny might make as one:
this product, greater than its sum.

Seven and-one-half millennia of exile.
Was she there for him to find?
Or was she only in his mind?
Was it always meant this way:
the swain to wander every day
and through each night, pursue his plight;
her being, always in his sight ...
Her sound ... His soul?

TO THE GODDESS WITHIN

Ancient seed of sleeping sky –
in vengeance, wrested from those thighs
of father, by a Titan son:
her sickle-handed sibling.
The goddess woke and woke the world
to fearsomeness and beauty.
Deep from shell-strewn temple bounds
she reigns and walks the world
in love and beauty awesome ...
Thus walking, lives the goddess –
wakes within us all.

* * *

I watch these walkers ...
And walking thus, watch I
these margins of her surging realm
stretched wide between the shore and sky
in majesty, with plumbless depths:
mere edges of that consciousness.
I love this space: this interface
that stretches to the sky ...
So, walking thus and watching thus,
walk I.

I watch in wonder ...
And wondering thus, watch I
the beauty of these fearsome depths:
vast surging of a consciousness
released upon our sphere of being
men and gods – mere instruments
of heaven's promptings; locked
in waking dreams and aspirations
suspended in the sky ...
So, wondering thus and dreaming thus,
watch I.

When you're withdrawn and at your ebb,
your temple lost in green depths –
your soughing whispers , 'I am here. This is no web,
for I am resident beyond the seagull's crying.
I am your body's element: the bearer of your soul.
I am the yin, your feminine: the truth to make you whole.
I come in beauty, come in love:
the content of your chalice ...
The half you lost and laid aside: your very grist and core.
I shore your soul and shoring thus,
your soul in shoaling, soars.'

JACK

My sprawling Jack-of-Frost
lays on his back; accosts
me with the tune
that hangs me from him.
He tunes the song he sings
from keepsakes lacking strings
or sounding-boards
for yesterday's illusions.

My scornful Jack-of-Frost
swings from my back and scoffs
about the lack
of rhyme or reason.
He reasons as he rants
about the obstacles of chance:
that steeplechase
of falls, and fate's contusions.

My robbing Jack-of-Grief
steals on me in my sleep
to render down
the turgid fats of reason.
He renders, as he paints
from the palette time acquaints
with aching wounds
and destiny's deep lesions.

My distant Jack-of-Reason
slips inside me out of season
to spread his tendrils gently
through my spine.
He thrusts his fingers deep
beneath the tissue of my sleep:
an alchemist
in anima confusions.

My whistling Jack-in-Season
rubs against me with good reason
as he modulates the passage of this song.
His melody now falters, as its tempo gently alters
and moves into a somewhat-minor key
of changes; chords well-tempered –
diminished but augmented ...
The theme its own, defying transposition.

Of all the Jacks-that-Gather
in these days, the one that matters
most of all, is that
of mocking Jack-of-Truth:
that prince of lost illusions
and price for thought transfusions
sees life, a leap of faith
not needing proof.

'A Box of Shells'

Rollerball & Wash on Arches Paper, 2014

AND YET THEY THANK HER

Just another scalp, on the belt
of the goddess moving fleet-foot
through the undergrowth –
sliding through the shadows
of ghosts and summers past ...
And, silent as the mists of morning,
melt and vanish in the cold
hard light of day.

Just another pelt, to charm
the waistline of a silent sylph,
moving with a grace
that time forgot; but not
forgotten by the bald ones
listing in her wake ...
No time could take from them
the hunger she so readily begot.

And yet they thank her;
for their baldness,
listing, hunger ...
Beg her, once again
to charm their senses;
take their skin
and wear it, for her own.

I HAD WONDERED

I had wondered, when you left
if words would dry
like leaves before their falling ...
If like the thoughts,
would tongue be cleft
and left to flounder – one lost wreck
stranded on the shoals
of summer's passage.

I have wondered, with you gone
if thoughts might fly
like leaves at autumn's calling ...
If with its call
would end our song –
as might migrate, the noble swan
leaving at the first
grey hint of winter.

I have wondered, in your void
if tongue would tie
like bells bereft of tolling ...
If in that lull,
of peal devoid
few means might be deployed
to warn of danger –
save life's barque from shoaling.

For I have laboured, in your wake
my voice to fly; this thirst to slake ...
The beast to name, that in my waking
hunts me in this undertaking -
breathing down my neck and days,
intent to rob from me the tune
hanging from my voice, consumed
by self-defeating torpor.

But I will yield no satisfaction
for the beast thrives on inaction ...
The roots and fruits his thrusting snout
grub out, are those of faith and doubt -
the faith to love, the doubt to leave ...
Twin yarns in the magician's sleeve
best separated on the loom
by reconfiguring fate's tune.

'Dragonfly at Dawn'
Rollerball & Wash on Arches Paper

MORNING PAGES

In the stillness and the breaking of the night,
stars wink out and daylight hums,
to draw from sleep – put dreams to flight.
The book lies open ... This day's life
awaiting substance from its source –
to draw from dreams, a present course.

Hordes throng the gates. The audience is restless –
all tickets paid, the cast arrayed in tatty splendour.
Both living and the dead cry out,
seek recognition from past doubts ...
Their meaning, cause, their tenure –
the mundane duties, must-be-dones,
the hopes, the dreams, the pleasures.

Aches and longings hang at bay,
aspirations pending. The quest remains
still-veiled in haze – its story, never-ending.
Procrastination clouds the mind, prevarication circling.
The clamour and the din increase ...
Where's comprehension, bringing peace?

In that awkwardness and finality of silence ...
Thoughts won't stop, while words won't come,
to still the brain's incessant hum.

MOONSHINE ALLEY

Almost moonshine alley
and the clunking, bamboo clatter
of the wind-chime stills the air
that drives the scudding white caps
through the sky ...

And hair that ruffles
in the madness, of the flight
down firefly highways
with the words that none dare whisper
to the night.

Listing moonshine galley
where staccato, tree-frogs stammer
as the wind-chime fills the air
that drives the scudding memories
from the sky ...

And fear that scuffles
with the sadness, of the flight
of gadfly byways
and the thoughts that come unbidden
to the night ...

Where thirsting memory mingles
with present tense ... The sense
that all things started and abandoned
to that flight, fell in a time
when all seemed ripe

And ready, to the touch of discontent –
when beckoning, firefly highways
gave way to gadfly byways
while meaningless distractions
drowned the air.

Almost moonshine alley
and the cheerful, bamboo chatter
of the wind-chime clears the air
that drives the scudding whitecaps
through the sky ...

And hair that ruffles
in the gladness, of the flight
of firefly highways
with the thoughts that one dares whisper
to the night.

DOWNPOUR IN THE CITY

Downpour in the city ...
And the solitary rainspout swells to overflowing,
spews its overburden without discrimination –
cuts a swathe that parts the wave
of lemming-borne umbrellas
beating a hasty crocodile retreat
from this sudden and most-unseasonable deluge.

Friday afternoon and a downpour in the city ...
The drumming din drowns out the traffic roar,
the maitre d', all idle conversation.
Lovers huddle, in sodden intimacy
along the café margins and downwind of the deluge,
trapped against the surging lemming tide
in abrupt, but not unwelcome, togetherness.

Hardly-hidden headlamps flaring,
skinny girls blaze their way, toward a virgin destiny –
while grim-faced shoppers,
Christmas clutched in one free arm,
brave this tide and scuttle, in a rush none understands –
basic seasonal programming
for scuttle bugs, who wend and weave their tenuous way ...
And still, the rainspout giant pisses on.

Accents jostle with the downpour din ...
Solemn matriarchs, with spouse in tow
(each, imports from some other place)
emerge in mild bewilderment,
intents at promenade now foiled.
Large-nosed girls, small breasts and teasing eyes
aflame with matching egos, breast this tide
to dance their tourist tango.

This is glorious! Buenos Aires must have been like this ...
When cafes thronged and spilled the streets,
while sudden and unseasonable downpours
fed, to fill the urgency of life;
where poets and rebels mingled with the heady
sweaty smell of rushing Friday afternoons –
pungent coffee, cigarettes, sudden rain and mobsters.

The cast and faces have not changed ...
Dark-suited businessmen, intent and sombre
feign ignorance of rain, full-focussed on their goals.
The timid girls with teasing eyes
dance and weave their breasting way
from their anonymous futures –
while tourist matrons, with spouse a-tow
(parcel-packing firsts of Season's Shoppers)
brave the dance of Friday city flights ...
And still, the solitary giant pisses on.

AS GRIEF'S FOR LOSS ...

As Grief's for loss, so Grief's a cross to bear;
through autumn's dreaming days, a course to share ...
Thus dreaming, grieve the passing of the years;
of friends, of youth, the wellspring's hopes and fears;
'til Grief herself becomes too much to bear –
engenders silence, thus to stem despair ...
Suspend the fall, the plight of flailing nights
which Grief bestows on all whom she ignites.

Thus grieved we all, the silent mute: this wall
pain raised about, as rampart to your fear ...
Not for yourself, but for the ones held dear –
and silenced thus, a clotted sanguine thrall
plied hidden bindings and with gag replete,
enforced a stillness, as such griefs accrete ...
Consigned to rest within a living tomb;
endure faux death, in antiseptic gloom.

There in the stillness, by that silence wrought
where sight and sound alone, accompany thought ...
And gates are shut on all which might be said –
where living bodies masquerade as dead;
where well-meant smiles deny what might be real;
unshielded words let slip, despite all zeal ...
Taunt, torture, torment, slip the knot of hope –
locked eyes, lashed ears: the bounds of your world's scope.

* * *

To languish not between two worlds, to hang
but storm the ramparts of the blood that sang
your grief to sleep the dream of no avail –
you summoned up your willpower, to prevail
and loose the bonds which held you in their keep,
turn back the flood, which fevered sanguine sleep ...
When grief alone is all that's left to ply,
some hope must filter through, to death decry.

To fade not through insistent failing night,
one spark alone was all it took to fight –
regain a hold on all your joys held dear,
turn back the flood of Grief, with purpose clear
and garner up a host of precious hours ...
But was it just for your joy, or for ours,
that time and tide retreated with those years
in laughter, more than in the stead of tears?

Retreat they did in part, but part alone,
as if the world in full, could not atone –
wipe out each blemish writ on history's page,
more hurts than could a second chance assuage ...
So passed your time, in anguish mixed with joy –
self-laughter, as the means to now deploy
to see your life (all lives), some cosmic joke
endured by all who labour in its yoke ...

And nearing end, the substance of those years
amount to what? Some hopes, some joys, some fears –
some aspirations never to be gained?
What cosmic joke, imperfectly-explained?
What might we take, when all is swept away
and clouds roll back, to show us our last day?
The stage is hushed – there will be no encore ...
So came your time, in time ... Then nothing more.

* * *

As Grief's to part, so Grief's the heart we bared
upon your leaving – for the times unshared,
lost to the past, lost to the times to come –
Grief is the loss, to which the rest succumb.
It's for the void, the absence and the fear –
the taking, for a reason still unclear:
the why and wherefore, of our little lives ...
The where and how and what? ... We hope, survives.

'Lost Dog Gothic'
Screenprint on Arches Dessin Paper, 1982.

A SONG OF YEARNING

In the belly of the world
there sleeps a dream, they but forgot.
The world remembers, knows and dreams –
a dream-song, spun from star to stream,
in shifting grass – the stillness of
a perfect dusk and dawn-washed clouds ...
The very breath of being.

Being – of a shifting dream
that all remember, save those in reason bred ...
In resonance of reason,
one waking dream, forgot.
And darkness builds ...
Ten thousand, thousand frames of light
in cities' darkness, glowing bright –
containments of each lost soul's dream
that stillness, in night's depth redeems.

In solitude, they hear it yet ...
The unsaid yearning, sense of loss –
that something, all have but, forgot.
Behind each window, glowing bright,
lone shadows move, linked by the night
and stirrings of vague memory –
of what? ... They know not what it meant,
before the fall – from consciousness and grace.

CONTRAST THIS WAVE

Contrast this wave of subsea spawning,
rushing for its shore, still dawning ...
Surging promises of doom,
visited on third-world shores,
leave its mark for evermore.

Homes and holdings, scant but precious,
swept aside, in tidal rush
and as this kraken retrogresses,
remnants wallow in the slush.
But Oh! But Oh! The human cost ...
The lives in one wet moment, lost!

The final score defies the count,
as hundreds, in their thousands mount.
These world-heard cries of inundation,
thrown out, from our Earth's poorest nations,
shock the ear, the heart, the mind ...
And still, the final death-toll climbs.

Contrast this wave, the aftermath –
as nations of the world take heart
and rush assistance, gifts of aid
to lands laid bare, by sea-born swathe ...
Save pestilence, wet-filth and thirst:
the horrors of the dead, the first to feel the rigours.

Calm descends – a people stunned,
count their dead, collect possessions:
so little left, from little ...
And simple lives, so simply lost –
lost forever, in the wash
of one great sweeping ripple.

Contrast this wave – this subsea spawn!

* * *

Contrast this storm, whose wave was born
to contrast brave humanity,
whose home became an inland sea –
locked by levees, might and substance ...
Still none might redeem them.

This, no surging behemoth
but harpies, venting all their wrath –
this storm swept all before her ...
A yielding ocean, gaining strength –
suppliant, followed down the length
of that great southern seaboard.

Prepared they were, precautions taken –
yet helpless still, stood by their nation,
watching devastation taking hold ...
Whilst hundreds, in their thousands fled,
still many, in their thousands dead,
are taken to the fold.

* * *

Contrast this wave, the days that follow ...
The great man, in sweet torpor wallows,
waiting for his moment.
In arrogance, he waits their plea –
whose home's become an inland sea ...
And Oh! And Oh! The Country's cost:
the property and oil drums lost!

Looting, plunder, rape and death –
bestowed on those these waters left.
Land of Plenty! Home of The Free!
Is this then, Prosper's Legacy ...
To foster Greed and Anarchy?

IN THE AFTERMATH

In the aftermath of plenty,
all the citadels of plenty fall
in clouds of death from which none crawl ...
Save those, who wail and beat the breast, to cry
that justice must be done, and justly so -
for innocents, (not innocence) were lost today ...
And innocents shall lose tomorrow.

In the aftermath of reason,
all the gods of reason gone ...
A brooding world, in madness waiting,
breeding such an undertaking.

The paper house of cards imploded,
as petals of decay unfolded,
stamens of their host, left crying -
heartbeat of a culture, dying ...
Pandemic, feasting on its host
as congress prayed to Holy Ghost.
And ganglions have taken hold,
in prophesies so long foretold
that thus, would end an era.

* * *

In the aftermath of horror,
barriers to horror fall, as packages of death arrive
in dust – designed to over-ride complacency and safety ...
The die-hard message rolls with ease –
the media, inured to please their audience of cult.

In the aftermath of avarice,
its culture, long-distended to bursting-point,
while strong anoint the 'have' and 'have-nots',
singled out, in lines of want
and wanting-not, defying comprehension ...
There's no small wonder, as this plunder
drives our earth, with all its worth,
to melt-down paranoia.

In the aftermath of carnage,
all vetoes placed on carnage fail ...
So might and freedom may prevail –
protect the world from further actions
practiced by ungodly factions: Pimpernels in Purdah.

* * *

The Coalition's hounds unleashed,
while stakes at play are now increased –
with theories of intrigue abounding,
preys they seek, elude their hounding ...
Resources tried, in vain they seek
to trap him, like a lover who
when passion (as it does), grows weak,
shape-changes to another.

In the aftermath of passion,
all first flush of passion fades ...
A brave new venue fills blue screens
with visions of night raids.

A brave new villain takes the stage –
the focus of this footage: game-boy war-games,
nightly-played ... No weapons found, the fiend's displayed,
dragged out from ravaged wreckage.
And vindicated now, they claim
(mythologies glossed over),
reluctant order is maintained – an interim,
so highly strained, as victors take possession.

In the aftermath of victory,
all sweet smell of victory flies ...
A new world order: friable,
fends off hints of lies.

In righteousness, the gods take seat
to meet once more, at Summit's peak -
assess the threat of terror.
And terror strikes, once more - again
(its echoes trembling through the glen) ...
Such was expected - just not when.
Thus galvanised, cold blood in thighs,
strict measures must be rendered -
quell freedoms, such as might give rise
to incidents, most-dreaded.

* * *

In the aftermath of terror,
all footholds found in freedom, slide -
most citizens have naught to fear
if citizens have naught to hide ...
Save those who fail and pay the cost,
of freedoms (for protection) lost ...
To languish in Orwellian dreams -
this world, no longer what once seemed.

'Microcosmos'
Screenprint on Arches Dessin Paper, 1984.

IT CAME UPON A MIDNIGHT CLEAR

It came upon a midnight clear
in hidden hymning, psalm and silent litany,
arising from the hearts of men,
unbidden and unvoiced ...
Lest doubt and fear should seize their hearts,
should hold dominion – make of might a mockery ...

The very gifts that set them free
to squander Man's impunity:
fragile rights that they in freedom
took for granted; held so dear –
that none but gods might beg their pardon;
of no thing else, have cause for fear.

It came upon a midnight clear:
from dawn 'til midnight, Media's means
flood the senses, fill mute heads
with doom-fraught litanies of fear ...
Pandemics, bombings, siren screams
exhort the world to fear and dread.

Awakened by this fear Man's bred,
an Earth alive (Man treats as dead) ...
Alive with power to end his scheming,
end the misuse, lack of care –
and, caring not for sirens screaming,
stirs, her warning to declare ...

'If fear and terror form Man's focus,
so they should, embrace his locus.
From the barrel, springs the fuse
that Man might use and so abuse
this Earth, which holds him dearly ...
To the well-spring, hangs the rope,
that Man might use to draw up hope
and mend his Earth sincerely.'

* * *

It came upon a midnight clear –
these times when fear, all else outsells,
make it a tool, laconic ...
From pills and potions, household spells,
to losing freedoms, rights held dear –
through forging rules draconic.

Fear is an instinct – in its place,
essential to the human race
(and every other creature)
but common use to sell coercion
every day, in every version
warps Man's very culture.

It's gross misuse, from pole to soul,
creates a world no longer whole.
In the portal, rests the key
all men may use to set all free,
to mend this world completely ...

In the Earth, resides the power
to drive the miscreant from his tower -
re-form this world discreetly.

* * *

It came upon a midnight clear,
that Man could sing a song of grace -
own his fear, and wear it with his clothing ...
Give it back its rightful place -
its image on cave walls adhere,
accepted, free of loathing.

If fear's misuse could be reduced,
Man's mother Earth might be induced
to still her restless stirrings ...
Reality's what Man creates
wherein his focus most relates,
through images recurring.

So sing, upon this midnight clear
a theme, its image to maintain,
of faith, in joy and beauty -
faith in the well-spring, to sustain ...
Belief, in one emboldened duty
to cherish Earth and hold her dearly,
proclaiming to the midnight clearly ...
There's naught to fear on Earth, but fear.

TIME SLIPS THE WARP

Time slips the warp, where time and timely place
co-mingle on the loom of space laid bare ...
And each thread slips the cloth where shadows fade
(the world seen edgewise in her strand of hair).
On my event horizon's interface
what now seems convex was before, concave ...
And all good reason and good sense efface.

Dual paradox within this field of grace,
twin singularities urge dreams to dare ...
And each dream slips the cloth that time upbraids
(the world lost edgewise in her dark-sunned pair).
On my event horizon's interface
all shadows cast and passed in space-time fade ...
And all good reason and good sense efface.

Time slips the warp, wherein her voice relates,
co-mingling on the loom that fate lays bare ...
And each word slips the cloth where dreams reside
(illusion lodging in a place none dares).
On my event horizon's interface
all boundaries of space and time subside ...
Each moment merging at one point of grace.

Twinned irises with depths where time abates,
turn in a dance no quantum could prepare ...
And each step strips the cloth, its fabric frayed
(the fool's an angel lacking cause to care).
On my event horizon's interface
assumptions of what's probable abrade ...
And all good reason and good sense efface.

Time slips the warp where time and seemly grace
entangle on the loom of space laid bare ...
And each move shifts the cloth the wise evade
(the fool lifts shadows where none others dare).
On my event horizon's interface
the vortex dancing in her eyes persuades
that all good reason and good sense efface.

MUTE CELLS CRY OUT

Mute cells cry out to catch again the dew,
call out the dawn, to free the fleeting night
as mute, they throng among the blessed few.

In silence, led by thirsts as they accrue
in waiting on this first spring's blush of light,
mute cells cry out to catch again the dew.

Dawn garners hope to feed the pulse, pursue
the promised hint of winter in its flight
as mute, they throng among the blessed few ...

Lean hillsides rush to herald with their hue,
spring's flush, as growing in their purpose, might
mute cells cry out to catch again the dew

and parched thirsts drink, neglected cells imbue
the residues of winter in its flight,
as mute, they throng among the blessed few.

Should seasons fail, their bright gifts then eschew ...
Still calling for a cause to give delight,
mute cells cry out to catch again the dew

and urge the hillsides, not to once subdue
relief, they found an instant in their sight
as mute, they throng among the blessed few.

While patiently, they wait again their cue
to welcome in a spring ablaze with might,
mute cells cry out to catch again the dew
as mute, they throng among the blessed few.

'Teddy and Rose'
Pencil on Cartridge Paper, 1976.

WHAT CAUSED THE STATESMEN ALL

What caused the statesmen all, to go away;
to leave affairs of state to rogues and fools
who build a future tainted by dismay,
foresight and wisdom absent from their tools?
What left us with so very little choice;
who at the ballots, is there to give hope
and through the shadows, guide us by their voice,
convince us, of abilities to cope?

Well-meaning men, believing they could fly
and finish hard, the race they chose to run,
too late, have found they ventured far too high,
their feathers softened, broken by the sun.
Where are the men of substance at the helm
whom greed or vanity shan't overwhelm?

RETRIEVAL FRAGMENT

To sleep within a bog, beneath a cairn:
the gift of being human – simply man.
But internment, in this tall and hollow log;
to rest, as some bright blazing totem;
to have such friends, as they would place
your remnants, borne aloft in grace –
as one, who shared not in their blood
but shared their brotherhood and love ...

To such degree, accord respect
with your remains, they might bedeck
and bear in sorrow deeply-felt ...
Within this tree trunk, held aloft;
embalmed within, inscribed without
in symbolism, scribed with pride ...
With language of this ancient race,
forever more, your soul embrace.

To be so loved, to be a part
of people's dreaming, sacred heart ...
This world should hold like reverence
for such superficial difference –
where sameness lives, beneath all skins
and all blood flows, from common springs.

REVISITING'S A TURNING IN THE MIND

Revisiting's a turning in the mind
to regions where mind ought not wish to go ...
To pace again, those paths akin in kind
to patterns we should, in good sense, now know.
Returning to the space which we once left;
repeating of the patterns we once knew -
is not designed to heal a soul bereft
nor lead us from a place we should eschew.

Re-written scripts replace the tapes we score ...
The moment moves on at an unseen pace;
brings comprehension we cannot ignore
in seeking out our own small point of grace.
Revisited's another time's tabloid ...
Read it with care or otherwise avoid.

'Maurie'
Conte Crayon on Fabriano Paper, 2015.

FOR MAURIE ... 15 OCTOBER 2006

A gentle soul once gently filled this space,
was known by all to some or more degree ...
Too late perhaps, we recognise his grace.

Bookshelf to bar and back, each day his pace
belied the truth that few might truly see ...
A gentle soul once gently filled this space.

Too often, kindness wears an unseen face,
consideration asks for no decree ...
Too late perhaps, we recognise his grace.

Though scorned or loved, some truths cannot efface
the truth that lived and loved for all to see ...
A gentle soul once gently filled this space.

So now he's gone and empty seems this place
he occupied so quietly and free ...
Too late perhaps, we recognise his grace.

It's often when one's gone without a trace,
we yearn to know the depths we did not see ...
A gentle soul once gently filled this space.
Too late perhaps, we recognise his grace.

HOW CAME WE TO THIS DARKNESS?

How came we to the darkness of this place again?
How leisurely the seams do fall apart
and frayed threads lose their grip on all that's bright ...
For bright you were - twice-met it seems ... Or more?

How swiftly-spent, the margins of the self do blur;
do shift the threads that bind them - shift and fade.
The carousel will turn, another blur descend the stair ...
A frozen moment played out for all time.

And so, to grief again we turn -
in sorrow's loss, the past to burn ...
But what should past become once more, the now;
encounter dragons, we had thought long-slain;
to find the dream, long-lost and spent ...
The present, one more stain?

How came we to the stillness of this place once more?
This instant's keening, lost again to time ...
One moment's keening song, the past to chide;
all efforts at a present: fresh - deride.

And swiftly-gone, the heartbreaks
and the loves long-spent;
infinity's swift instant, evermore ...
For some, life is a moment from the past, replayed.
The carnival's mad frenzy writes the score.

'Over Sir John's Wood'

Pencil Study for Screenprint, 1980.

TWIN EAGLES RISE

Twin eagles rise through half-light skies;
chase late November's sullen afternoon
to drop, bank, soar ... To sweep and rise again –
grace dusk-stained embers of this fading day
with winds just right, to bear the might
of wedge-tailed majesty ... And death.

Death on a rising updraft, glides
and soars above this last-light valley:
last for one, whose end has come ...
Mute benediction, signed in stealth
and shifting shadows, in the blush –
last flush, of gold and crimson on the hills.

Death down the spiralling updraft slides,
drawn through the five-hued talons of his eyes
to the prey who waits him, calls him down –
tolled by the knell the cattle wear ...
At forest edge, on hillock's last illumined rise,
sudden and unseen, drops death.

The hill falls still, as homeward-cattle-bound
peal out the ending of another day – and life;
a lowing hymn marks out their hoof-steps,
deep and mild. Light fades ...
The updrafts falter and are gone –
gone too, these pinioned majesties on air.

SONG FOR A FLAT WORLD

They told me that the world be flat;
that there be dragons
and after them, be monsters.
Venture past a certain point ...
All else will fall away.

Yet, like reborn Columbus,
I've set my sails and headed east ...
One compass bearing, all I need -
some landfall ... And the promise
where a sought-for, new world calls.

Fair such skies as beckon, lead
into the grail-lit morning;
and fair the song the trade winds sing
so softly, through our rigging;
and fair, the course that's set -

and fair, the seas to follow ...
Some landfall on a promised shore,
beyond the flat-edge world.
Dare to venture past this point ...
All else will fall away.

YOU ARE MY SONG

You are my evening and my autumn song
and you would be the last I'd wish to sing;
as autumn moves to winter, short or long –
I'll sing you still, whatever time might bring.
I'll sing your song with passion and with joy,
with tenderness and sweet gentility ...
And if time's passage should that voice destroy,
your melody will linger clear and free.

Should you consent to hold me and my love
against your heart and ear for all of time,
your song, your name, will charge my heart above
all others and to yours, my voice will climb.
For you remain my substance, my delight –
you are the song that fills me, day and night.

I THINK YOU HAVE, MY HEAD UNDONE

I think you have, my head undone;
by all that's light and all that's bright -
I know, my heart, you've overrun ...

For as your landfall hove in sight,
you furled my sails, some twelve months past -
with all your light, by all that's bright.

Though rush our days and seasons past,
moored in these new world's waters sound,
you've furled my sails, these twelve months past.

Much goodness, from your soul rebounds
and in your presence, I am blessed -
moored in these waters, safe and sound.

I know you have, my heart possessed -
yours is the grail, that brings me light
and by your presence, I am blessed.

You show me beauty, as my right;
I feel you have, my past undone.
Yours is the grail, that lights my night ...
I know, my heart, you've overrun.

FOUR YEARS HAVE COME TO US

Four years have come to us and washed these shores,
as varied as the tides, which in their surge
bear mostly treasured shells and little more ...

We've seen our journeys into one converge,
despite rare storm-front surges from the past
as varied as the tides, which by us, surge ...

Our voyage, mainly smooth beneath this mast –
astern, the gentle passage of each now,
in spite of storm-front surges from our pasts.

Since setting sail, four years have passed our bow,
to run our length and sparkle in our wake,
as churns astern, the passing of each now ...

The purpose of this journey's no mistake;
so we must trim our sails, and fair seas urge
to run our length and sparkle in our wake ...

For right a voyage is, that would so merge,
while years may come to us and wash our shores ...
Then, as we trim our sails and fair seas urge,
find mainly pretty shells and little more.

ONE SEASON'S MOULD

Vinegar! ... And cloves! ...
For weeks it's rained - or seems so,
as the last of summer's breath lies heavy;
burdens every mote that ever settled
on the contours of my home ...
And spores spring forth in sudden places.

An Host is come ...
Entrenched its mould-spawned minions;
encamped itself on bulwark and in hollow;
laid siege - established beachheads
on my walls, my couch, my shoes, my belts!
This pungent, rotting-citrus bloom springs forth -
adorns them all.

In the village,
townsfolk mutter - curse and throng the streets;
storm shelves of pharmacy and hardware both,
for oil of cloves and vinegar;
regroup, for bleach in every form,
as desiccator vendors rub their hands, and dehumidifiers
thrum, to drain the hub of humid households.

These then, are the wages
of our mountaintop existence,
lodged along the margins of the clouds ...
Responding to the fungal fugue, with seasonal insistence,
we air our cupboards, stoke our fires –
maintain the mushroom vigilance,
our treasures to preserve.

'Mushrooms at Mapleton'
Rollerball & Wash on Arches Paper, 2006.

MUTE SUNFLOWERS FROM GREY ASHES

Mute sunflowers from grey ashes sadly rise,
their benedictions, begging time to stall ...
To see how reason, from this world still flies.

So brief the time they had to realise,
that time could end thus and bright darkness fall,
whilst mute, would sunflowers from grey ashes rise.

For in that instant, stripped of compromise -
a final moment, from which none might crawl;
none witness for themselves, how reason flies.

These scattered parts - confetti of their lives,
adorn the landscape ... Silence to appall,
as mutely, sunflowers from sad ashes rise.

For while we argue, where the true blame lies,
news networks vie, to hold us in their thrall;
convey how reason, from this world now flies.

Until another headline sounds its cries
and interests in the current banner pall,
mute sunflowers will, from ashes, sadly rise
to show how reason, from this world still flies.

'Potted Plant, Mt Gravatt'
Pastel on Cartridge Paper, 1977.

AS AUTUMN TURNS ...

As autumn turns, to sleep with winter's years
and friends recede, as hailed by close of day,
we seek distractions to allay our fears
that in the end, we're little more than clay.
We look for what we might now leave behind -
convince ourselves that we might be revered;
that much of it was not just in our mind
but had a form, more valued than was feared.

Spare us from dwelling in a pumped-up past,
reliving blown-out visions of our youth:
false vanities, devoid of power to last -
mythologies, which test the bounds of truth.
Wear old age with such modesty and grace,
vain foolishness in old age shan't deface.

A SONNET FOR VALENTINE'S

This February has arrived, while still
our own fleet hares return to laze and graze
the ever-constant haven of our hill.
Through mists and squall, they've come to grace this slope
and brought their young to share these joyous days
which crown their own existence with such hope.

This week has seen them sportive, gay and light;
to leap, spin, turn, cavort across the hill
in mating-mad abandonment's fey flight
to garner all these joys at summer's end –
ward off the threat of hoary winter's chill ...
Such is the essence of the path I'd wend
to tarry with you for this little while
and give you some cause, through the mists to smile.

'Genet à Kemp'
Monoprint on Japanese Rice Paper, 1981.

TO LATER FRIENDSHIPS

Friends come and go throughout the flux of life;
they catch the sun to shine and briefly flare
but often, overtaken by life's shade,
they find themselves replaced by other cares ...
These mostly not for reasons false or trite
but simply time and distance lets them fade.
Nostalgia meanwhile, holds them in her arms
to hang around our life like chain-linked charms.

And then, there are those others, coming late
as sparks to smoulder in the embers of our day;
who through their strengths will suffer no such fate -
for you, my friend, will sidestep all the shade
wherein, for time and distance, others laid ...
Thus unforgotten, ever shall you stay.

ON DISTANT DOGGY DOTAGE

Viewed up close, each wall becomes a portal
to other worlds: a dim reality, mislaid.
Frozen in time, he becomes the new Zen master
focused on infinity, while paint films melt and fade.

Locked in satori's bright embrace – this empty dog-bowl:
watershed of nothingness, beyond all expectations.
Frozen thus he'll stand, eye to wall, at thresholds
of infinity in none-ness ... Never being there at all.

His days turn on this wheel of life, swinging; where
eats and sleep form his meridian; guide his bearings –
always to dream ... And dream, he does ...
There to sit or stand, soft eyelids drooping
and then full-suddenly, to slump ...
Yawn – lick his chops ... Then slump again.

He perambulates in old man gait, oscillating
between arthritic waddle and pure puppy-manic –
walking uphill under heavy load, where one shake
will send loose legs all scattering ...
Leaves before his Autumn wind,
dispatched to cardinal points in one slipped instant –
old man locomotion and all traction, lost.

Oscillates on sounding of the tea bell – reverts
from plodding senior, to bright show-pony manic
in one eye's blinking, legs all a-skitter
round about and under the high-borne food bowl ...
There to leap and dance high galliards of joy:
anxiety's relief, when She-who-must-be-loved
returns with bowl, to boon some treat.

And, thus-rewarded for his patience,
he'll have the last word, with a pee
in unexpected places mostly – and, with stress removed,
drift off to dream enlightenment again.

Perhaps all dotage holds such realms of shadow,
lost in light ... Where eyesight blurs;
where hearing fades; and cunning of the old
lights all such hidden places, in a twilight of the senses
not all what it might seem ...
Where faux farragoes of decrepitude
are bound to triumph every time.

'Benji – Studies at Hervey Bay'
Charcoal pencil on Cartridge Paper, 2015.

SEVENTEEN-SEVENTY OBSERVED

With melting-down of day across our bay,
this languid air exhales and stills its breath ...
if for an instant. Vain though it might try
to hold day's pulse in check,
an impulse to inhale, at length gives way ...

So breathe it does – the very bay to tremor
in this late day's holy, speckled blaze ...
the curtains stir and bougainvillea quiver.

Across the bay, the coastal sand-dunes haze,
lost in the build of shimmering sea-alight,
where mirrored rippling blinds and sears the eyes
as setting sun sparks water to ignite ...
in brilliance, burning bright enough to daze.

Our atmosphere is charged, light breezes gather ...
tremble ... and on our Naked Bow, all sways
as dusk-bent stirrings herald forth cool weáther.

Sun setting on bay's rim, one moment flares ...
igniting far-flung ranges still in reach
while closer, water with its coastline fades –
as mute, the open arms of evening stretch
a fast embrace, to hold all in her shades.

Night settles in and then all pales.
The stars and mooring lights switch on.
The bay breathes in – day's light is gone
and all about, our earth exhales.

'My Father's Father, Herbert Drew, 1915'
Conte Crayon & Compressed Charcoal on Cartridge Paper, 2013.

MY FATHER'S GHOST IS SLEEPING

My Father's ghost is sleeping on the stairs -
the attic air is musty with his heat.
    Heir to his chaptered blood,
I recognise the scent of reason's breath
and navigate the corridors that bleed
this sap of singularity ... His heirs.

My Mother's brother's eyes gaze back from home,
to burn me through the confines of the glass.
    With incandescent eye ...
From mirrors and shop windows as I pass,
he mocks all futile efforts made to flee
the stamp of blood, fixed firm within the stone.

My Mother keeps her silence to herself -
just hums and smiles discretely from the hearth.
    With patience and with love,
she stands aside ... To murmur through the breath
contained within the stone, the stair, the blood,
that all is as it should be ... Such is life.

Late afternoon's shaft filters through the slats -
lights up each mote of dust upon the sill ...
    Illumined shards long-gone
come present ... Gather likewise, for us all -
reminders of the blood stored in the stone ...
My Father's ghost is stirring, as he sleeps upon the stairs.

I WOULD, IF COULD, SING UNTO YOU ...

I would, if could, sing unto you a season
before the joy of innocence was lost;
before these times of binary-fostered reason
burnt bridges, rationality had crossed.

I'd grant us all a season in much simpler times;
a season long before the web was spun ...
where urgent self-promotion had no walls to climb -
when time was leisurely, no race to run.

I'd sing you slow perfection's Christmas tidings:
a carol crafted lovingly with joy;
no settling for the fast-fix now abiding ...
some thoughtful patient savour to employ.

So as we move now through another Season
let's strive for balance in this fledgeling reason.

'Struggling Plant at Hervey Bay'
Notebook Sketch with Charcoal Pencil, 2015.

CHRISTMAS COMES BUT ONCE A YEAR

Christmas comes but once a year.
Again it's caught me unawares.
I'd thought it safe to say, 'It's near'
then muse ahead, what words to share
but time fooled me – and suddenly it's here!

Yes, suddenly The Day is here.
I'd thought once more, some verse to write
to hail this Season loud and clear
and sing sweet greetings – nothing trite,
to fill your Christmas morn with cheer ...

Yes, fill your Christmas morn with cheer.
Instead, I pour this drivel out
as doggerel, whose form I fear
and scorn in others' word-some bouts
which warrant not the term, 'sincere'.

But Christmas does come once a year
and though our Range dawns bright or drear,
my love for you is always here.
Your presence in my life is dear –
and near to me, my heart you cheer.

WE DWELL IN THE HOUR OF PERFIDY

We dwell in the hour of perfidy –
of smiling mouth, averted eye;
of singular ambition spent
for the season politic ...
subversion's lie.

Old bodkin's friend, well-armed and girt
with promise and the well-plied lie –
whose honeyed lips drip the garden's kiss,
as waiting surrogates stand by
the doors to opportunity and power.

No hallowed halls so reeked of trust
abandoned to the must and dust,
ambition laid so thickly on their walls.

We dwell in the hours of perfidy and greed;
to turn our backs on empathy and need –
while dreams of reason politic
with binary intent,
all other truths belie.

Here, in unseen quarters of the world,
Orwellian drum-rolls sound the hour;
mark the beating of a culture spent
and passing of intelligence lament –
with Huxley's breath, descending down its days.

Narcissi bloom beside each stream,
to nod their heads, in discourse self-contained –
while busy fingers thumb each screen,
mute-slavish to a culture rent by social discourse:
slow advents all, to anarchy in reason.

'Mere treachery!' the traitors cry, lulling us to sleep ...
whilst in the glow of evening screens,
by other options, urged to dreams
of avarice and winning come what may –
we trade our minds.

In perfidies we thrive and throng,
as each new trinket croons the song
distraction needs, to guarantee our slumber.

THE CROW ('CORVUS MULTIFACETUS')

Stark, dark and sometimes sonorous: The Crow -
harshly the grumble, gently to chuckle and mutter;
funereal - to strut and stride about his stage
(for all the world's his own to fill) ...
wherein to bleat and caw his way through life.

For want of song, chants dolorous complaint
with studied reverence ... to terminate each sermon
with considered, drawn-out 'Aaaaawws!'
Whereon, forgetting what he really meant to say,
he'll start again to recommence his caw.

Occasionally, he'll toss sardonic humour in,
to bounce, hop, jump and skip awhile
(but not too much, mind you) ...
we must maintain our gravitas
with solemnity, in undertaker roles.

When all is done, he'll settle softly with his mate
to chat together, rest awhile ... to chuckle
at her jokes and 'Chuk-Chuk!' oh so gently
in her dark mysterious ear.

The raven, crow, the rook and jackdaw
abide the wide world over, to knock
at poets' doors in dead of night ...
there, 'Nevermore!' to whisper, through the confines
of the dark - and mock the tossing sleeper in his plight.

They feast on death about the roadsides;
leave no blood-bright corpse unturned ...
cadavers grant them nourishment and joy.
They scorn unwary drivers, as they set about their meal,
reluctant to break from their carrion zeal.

Their reputation tarnished by the prejudice of myth –
they bear the burden lodging in their eye ...
with steady glare, they challenge all to fear
death's chill and ready doom, gazed down
from lonely fenceposts or the carapace of tombs.

In spite of all bad-press, they're a most congenial lot
when gathered round in numbers of their own.
Omnivorous, they are in truth, living simply on their wits,
whilst taking care in sharing family chores.

They're clever and resourceful – quite adept at forging tools;
intelligent ... as mimics, highly skilled.
They're family people, dedicated fully to their task
whilst sharing through their cross-talk, dawn to dusk.

So look upon them softly, as you take their chatter in.
They're not the stark dark harbingers of doom.
They're simply nature's cleaners, in pursuit of nature's awe –
to quantify her beauty, with their starkly clarion caw.

'Frank'
Compressed Charcoal on Newsprint, 2001.

THE BRUSHES AND THE PENS, ARE STILL AND SILENT ...

The brushes and the pens, are still and silent now.
The pastels and the chalks, are fast asleep –
all hue and cry of pencils, rendered mute.

No more, the gleeful gestures of this fertile mind –
the florid fancies of his inward eye, no more
to grace, the reams of papers gathered here.

The mimic and the wit, have had their day –
the lightfast humour vented, soon would fade
and dusk come down, to dim where daylight glowed.

But still the reel keeps turning, while the stories flicker on
and ever in the background, ring the songs
of Louii, Frankie, Tony, Ella – every jazz-bound Great.

Bright stars in heaven now claim him as their own ...
The myriad of loves he held, pursued him to the end
and left their imprint here for all to see – how fevered
burnt this candle, through its much too, far short life.

ONCE MORE, I FIND I'M TAKEN BY SURPRISE

Once more, I find I'm taken by surprise
as Christmas rushed in quickly, once again.
We've been so busy watching cloudless skies,
I'd overlooked the need to prime my pen
whilst wondering, if it would rain ... and when.

It will rain sometime – question is, 'Just when?'
This year we need it more than we have most,
with weathers taking on a nasty spin ...
where fires rage; homes, animals, are lost –
while politicians juggle all their costs

With scant regard for common people's costs ...
where smoke and mirrors cloud the light of day;
obscure the rights and liberties fast lost
and still, the droughts and fires, come what may.
The best that they can offer is to pray.

In spite of dire disaster, I would pray
you health and happiness, for all our years ...
surmount all obstacles to come our way –
bring light of hope to banish any fears
while Christmas times ring joys, so loud and clear.

THERE CAME A TIME ...

There came a time when man was sent to trial ...
For squandered excess, too long fuelled his greed -
forever wrapped his days in blind denial.

A pestilence born, some would say from vials -
the virus spread its spawned, almighty seeds
to bring a time when man was brought to trial.

Time's hands, long-chasing midnight on earth's dial,
as many still pretended, 'There's no need.' ...
Forever wrapping ways in blind denial.

Man's growth in numbers challenged reason's cavel -
consumption's wants, the basis for their creed ...
So came a time, when all was put on trial.

The spreading of the pathogen went viral
when magnified by public media's speed –
all rationale lost, in some blind denials.

With commonsense fast lost, the cry, 'Survival!'
rebounded through most shopping malls, to feed
new times, where courtesies were put to trial.

As weeks turned into months beyond retrieval,
mortalities mount higher and exceed
all figures leaders gauged, in their denials.

Then finally, amidst this wreckage global,
humanity took stock and sought to heed
the lessons learnt, when they were sent to trial ...
Forever wrapped in dreams of blind denial.

A LOCKDOWN SONNET

Another day of musing, what to do next,
became the battlecry across the land ...
With only so much news that one might text,
this isolation's getting out of hand.

The boredom and the ennui are so deadly
and jigsaw vendors watch their profits grow -
all brief encounters, seen as most ungodly ...
The social web, its slipstream in full flow.

What will it take, to take us back to normal?
Will normal, ever be the norm again?
Is it likely that this thing could have a sequel?
Are we always on the knife-edge, until then?

What made us think that we could rule this planet?
We're simply pawns, in mortal roles, God dammit!

'Richmond Hill, 1975'
Notebook Sketch: Aquarelle graphite stick and wash.

BRIGHT AND SHINING ...

Bright and shining was the cup she bore
but its bowl wore a tarnish under.
Glowing and soft was the skin she wore
to strike him with awe and wonder.
And full-well he knew, that when she left
the world that he knew would soon be cleft,
leaving his years rent asunder.

Silken and soft was the cloth she wove
and its threads held his undoing.
True and constant the heart he gave,
all other claims eschewing.
In time, time flew and a distance leapt
into the space that his pulse had swept
far from the other's knowing.

Years, then decades, would at length run on
while the weft would become unravelled –
the dream once dreamed, now a dream long gone
with its byways no longer travelled ...
Until all that remained was an afternoon claimed,
where the red deer stood still out on Richmond Hill
and while the boys' kites and hawks were high flying –
and a gentle caress sent in motion, the test
when the slow wheels of fate were set turning.

RANDOM NOTES ON THE POEMS

A poem should stand independantly on its own feet (whether they be iambic, trochaic, anapaestic or otherwise). An attempt to fully-explain specific poems, will risk sucking the very life out of them ... as well also, might an overly-pedantic insistence on grammatical correctness. One has to concede though, that from an historical viewpoint in particular, there are works formed in verse where some readers might, sometime along in the future, benefit in their appreciation by having access to a key of the most fundamental nature, to allow for that first tumbler in the lock of comprehension to drop into place, thereby opening the door to something which one might otherwise look upon, as being of too arcane an exercise.

I must confess to owning an overt, pervading fondness for metaphor and allegory in my writing. For those who look for no-frills simplicity, I apologise but make no excuses, since I find no poetic virtue in being more than obvious -that is not the raison d'être of poetry. On occasion though, a clue to place the work in some sort of context, can make all the difference in successfully communicating with one's audience. A poem eventually, should be legible in some fashion, and it is with this intent, that I leave the door slightly ajar on some few of the works in this selection ...

SOME OCCASIONAL POEMS TO NOTE:

[19] 'TRAIN: EIGHT-THIRTY PADDINGTON TO PLYMOUTH' ... More of a simple, historical curiosity here. The year is 1977, London and I have read in recent weeks, Allen Ginsberg's epic train-travel poem of eleven years earlier, 'Iron Horse'. I have come late in discovering Ginsberg and in these times, he still impresses many of our generation. I find myself taking my own train journey, while on business, to Exeter: a regular event, but for today, with no extraneous company ... and in a pensive mood, I muse.

[43] 'AS GRIEF'S FOR LOSS' ... The year is 1999 and our mother falls prey to a massive stroke – after the same fashion as the French journalist and editor of Elle magazine, Jean Dominique Bauby, five years earlier. Both found themselves the subject of 'locked-in syndrome' ... unable to move or communicate whilst remaining fully conscious and aware. Bauby, through his one operable eye and a dedicated assistant from his former staff, managed to write a powerful memoir, 'The Diving Bell and The Butterfly', simply by blinking in a pre-emptive text fashion; all before shortly dying on its completion, as some sort of very dramatic denouement. I personally, watched my mother forge her way out of her similar, imposed prison, by creating her own alternate neural paths, initially through the strength of her inner willpower alone. Where Bauby fell short, she managed to return to the world for a sufficient time to escort my father into a safer place for his own final years. It is now mid-2002.

[49] 'CONTRAST THIS WAVE' ... Boxing Day, 2004 and an earthquake in the Indian Ocean gives birth to a tsunami family of waves, with a horrifying death toll in Banda Aceh and other heavily-populated centres throughout the region. Fast forward eight months and Atlantic seaboards of the southern United States are devastated by a wave of inland flooding, generated by a massive tropical storm, Hurricane Katrina. The responses of the world and respective governments of the time, along with the preoccupations of those individual governments, with the attendant effects of these two waves are markedly different – one, with a most disappointingly low level of apparent indifference and a reticence to act.

[52] 'IN THE AFTERMATH' ... 11th September 2001 and the United States are attacked on home soil, in a horror to be remembered for all time, simply as 9/11. The true facts will perhaps remain obscured by everlasting questions, which fade in peoples' memories as the years obscure them but still, it happened, and in the days afterwards, a poem was commenced ... and then, midway, stalled ... not knowing where it was to go next but knowing the story to be incomplete. Two years of retaliations passed, as first Afghanistan, and then Iraq were invaded under a mix of guises - but always with heavy visual reportage and updates on most television screens, most evenings across the planet. And then there came a day, when that unfinished, by now semi-epic poem found its denouement.

[65] 'WHAT CAUSED THE STATESMEN ALL' ... A Shakespearean Sonnet which speaks for itself. Suffice it to say, that it was prompted by the dilemma of where to place one's selections on the ballot paper, on the eve of the Queensland state election, late in 2007.

[67] 'RETRIEVAL FRAGMENT' ... Sometime in 2008, a television documentary deals with the tragic passing of a helicopter pilot in Arnhem Land, NT. Whilst not himself indigenous, he had selflessly-served, and was dearly loved by, the indigenous communities whom he tended there for many years - a touching tale, transcending racial differences.

[83] 'MUTE SUNFLOWERS FROM GREY ASHES' ... July, 2014 and Malaysia Airlines Flight 17 (MH17), on route from Amsterdam to Kuala Lumpur, is shot down whilst flying over eastern Ukraine, close to the Russian border, by pro-Russian troops. All 298 passengers and crew are killed and little remains, other than a widely-scattered field of mixed human, personal and mechanical debris, spread over a vast area of countryside.

[90] 'ON DISTANT DOGGY DOTAGE' ... Requiring no commentary but well-deserving of this tender dedication. A beloved pet, Benji, came via my partner and latter muse, Christine, and endeared himself through the ensuing years. The prettiest Havanese-Bichon terrier ... noisy, always fraught with separation anxiety, feisty, coprophagous, silken-soft with a high-waisted stylish figure and a sweet, expressive face - nothing short of a veritable chick-magnet - as the expression for handsome dogs goes. Nursed gently through his latter years of dotage, he finally, sadly succumbed to age one day around his seventeenth year and will remain forever, sorely-missed.

[105] 'THE BRUSHES AND THE PENS ARE STILL AND SILENT ... November, 2019, a true human being is released from his growing physical bondage of very many years and sets off, having shuffled off his own sadly-worn-out mortal coil. Nothing more is required, beyond a heartfelt dedication to a dear friend of forty-plus years, Frank Moffatt – a lifetime artist and hugely-entertaining author for children and the child who lives in all of us ... a prolific and colourful imagination, never to be stilled nor contained, he leaves an enormous void.

[107] 'ONCE MORE, I FIND I'M TAKEN BY SURPRISE' ... 2019, a Christmas poem – and for that particular year, no more need be said.

[108] 'THERE CAME A TIME' ... 2020, the year of Covid19 and the birth of the pandemic. This tribute, in the form of an extended Villanelle, a classic format, strikingly appropriate on similar sombre occasions, seemed a fitting form in which to offer commentary.

[111] 'A LOCKDOWN SONNET' ... 2020 once more, and the trials and social pressures of the pandemic's lockdowns demand further classic presentation, this time by way of the Shakespearean Sonnet in full flight. And as 'Hamlet' ends, his final cut-short line ... 'The rest is silence.'

www.ingramcontent.com/pod-product-compliance
Lightning Source LLC
Chambersburg PA
CBHW060756310726
48980CB00002B/112

* 9 7 8 0 6 4 5 4 7 0 1 2 3 *